I0158009

The Poetry of Algernon Charles Swinburne

VOLUME XVIII – VARIOUS POEMS

Algernon Charles Swinburne was born on April 5th, 1837, in London, into a wealthy Northumbrian family. He was educated at Eton and at Balliol College, Oxford, but did not complete a degree.

In 1860 Swinburne published two verse dramas but achieved his first literary success in 1865 with Atalanta in Calydon, written in the form of classical Greek tragedy. The following year "Poems and Ballads" brought him instant notoriety. He was now identified with "indecent" themes and the precept of art for art's sake.

Although he produced much after this success in general his popularity and critical reputation declined. The most important qualities of Swinburne's work are an intense lyricism, his intricately extended and evocative imagery, metrical virtuosity, rich use of assonance and alliteration, and bold, complex rhythms.

Swinburne's physical appearance was small, frail, and plagued by several other oddities of physique and temperament. Throughout the 1860s and 1870s he drank excessively and was prone to accidents that often left him bruised, bloody, or unconscious. Until his forties he suffered intermittent physical collapses that necessitated removal to his parents' home while he recovered.

Throughout his career Swinburne also published literary criticism of great worth. His deep knowledge of world literatures contributed to a critical style rich in quotation, allusion, and comparison. He is particularly noted for discerning studies of Elizabethan dramatists and of many English and French poets and novelists. As well he was a noted essayist and wrote two novels.

In 1879, Swinburne's friend and literary agent, Theodore Watts-Dunton, intervened during a time when Swinburne was dangerously ill. Watts-Dunton isolated Swinburne at a suburban home in Putney and gradually weaned him from alcohol, former companions and many other habits as well.

Much of his poetry in this period may be inferior but some individual poems are exceptional; "By the North Sea," "Evening on the Broads," "A Nympholept," "The Lake of Gaube," and "Neap-Tide."

Swinburne lived another thirty years with Watts-Dunton. He denied Swinburne's friends access to him, controlled the poet's money, and restricted his activities. It is often quoted that 'he saved the man but killed the poet'.

Swinburne died on April 10th, 1909 at the age of seventy-two.

Index of Contents

ATHENS: AN ODE

Ere from under earth again like fire the violet kindle,   [Strophe 1.
Ere the holy buds and hoar on olive-branches bloom,
Ere the crescent of the last pale month of winter dwindle,
Shrink, and fall as falls a dead leaf on the dead month's tomb,
Round the hills whose heights the first-born olive-blossom brightened,
Round the city brow-bound once with violets like a bride,
Up from under earth again a light that long since lightened
Breaks, whence all the world took comfort as all time takes pride.
Pride have all men in their fathers that were free before them,
In the warriors that begat us free-born pride have we:
But the fathers of their spirits, how may men adore them,
With what rapture may we praise, who bade our souls be free?
Sons of Athens born in spirit and truth are all born free men;
Most of all, we, nurtured where the north wind holds his reign:
Children all we sea-folk of the Salaminian seamen,
Sons of them that beat back Persia they that beat back Spain.
Since the songs of Greece fell silent, none like ours have risen;
Since the sails of Greece fell slack, no ships have sailed like ours;
How should we lament not, if her spirit sit in prison?
How should we rejoice not, if her wreaths renew their flowers?
All the world is sweeter, if the Athenian violet quicken:
All the world is brighter, if the Athenian sun return:
All things foul on earth wax fainter, by that sun's light stricken:
All ill growths are withered, where those fragrant flower-lights burn.
All the wandering waves of seas with all their warring waters
Roll the record on for ever of the sea-fight there,

When the capes were battle's lists, and all the straits were slaughter's,
And the myriad Medes as foam-flakes on the scattering air.
Ours the lightning was that cleared the north and lit the nations,
But the light that gave the whole world light of old was she:
Ours an age or twain, but hers are endless generations:
All the world is hers at heart, and most of all are we.

Ye that bear the name about you of her glory,   [Antistrophe 1.
Men that wear the sign of Greeks upon you sealed,
Yours is yet the choice to write yourselves in story
Sons of them that fought the Marathonian field.
Slaves of no man were ye, said your warrior poet,
Neither subject unto man as underlings:
Yours is now the season here wherein to show it,
If the seed ye be of them that knew not kings.
If ye be not, swords nor words alike found brittle
From the dust of death to raise you shall prevail:
Subject swords and dead men's words may stead you little,
If their old king-hating heart within you fail.
If your spirit of old, and not your bonds, be broken,
If the kingless heart be molten in your breasts,
By what signs and wonders, by what word or token,
Shall ye drive the vultures from your eagles' nests?
All the gains of tyrants Freedom counts for losses;
Nought of all the work done holds she worth the work,
When the slaves whose faith is set on crowns and crosses
Drive the Cossack bear against the tiger Turk.
Neither cross nor crown nor crescent shall ye bow to,
Nought of Araby nor Jewry, priest nor king:
As your watchword was of old, so be it now too:
As from lips long stilled, from yours let healing spring.
Through the fights of old, your battle-cry was healing,
And the Saviour that ye called on was the Sun:
Dawn by dawn behold in heaven your God, revealing
Light from darkness as when Marathon was won.
Gods were yours yet strange to Turk or Galilean,
Light and Wisdom only then as gods adored:
Pallas was your shield, your comforter was Pæan,
From your bright world's navel spake the Sun your Lord.

Though the names be lost, and changed the signs of Light and Wisdom be,   [Epode 1.
By these only shall men conquer, by these only be set free:
When the whole world's eye was Athens, these were yours, and theirs were ye.
Light was given you of your wisdom, light ye gave the world again:
As the sun whose godhead lightened on her soul was Hellas then:
Yea, the least of all her children as the chosen of other men.
Change your hearts not with your garments, nor your faith with creeds that change:
Truth was yours, the truth which time and chance transform not nor estrange:

Purer truth nor higher abides not in the reach of time's whole range.
Gods are they in all men's memories and for all time's periods,
They that hurled the host back seaward which had scourged the sea with rods:
Gods for us are all your fathers, even the least of these as gods.
In the dark of days the thought of them is with us, strong to save,
They that had no lord, and made the Great King lesser than a slave;
They that rolled all Asia back on Asia, broken like a wave.
No man's men were they, no master's and no God's but these their own:
Gods not loved in vain nor served amiss, nor all yet overthrown:
Love of country, Freedom, Wisdom, Light, and none save these alone.
King by king came up against them, sire and son, and turned to flee:
Host on host roared westward, mightier each than each, if more might be:
Field to field made answer, clamorous like as wave to wave at sea.
Strife to strife responded, loud as rocks to clangorous rocks respond
Where the deep rings wreck to seamen held in tempest's thrall and bond,
Till when war's bright work was perfect peace as radiant rose beyond:
Peace made bright with fruit of battle, stronger made for storm gone down,
With the flower of song held heavenward for the violet of her crown
Woven about the fragrant forehead of the fostress maiden's town.
Gods arose alive on earth from under stroke of human hands:
As the hands that wrought them, these are dead, and mixed with time's dead sands:
But the godhead of supernal song, though these now stand not, stands.
Pallas is not, Phoebus breathes no more in breathing brass or gold:
Clytæmnestra towers, Cassandra wails, for ever: Time is bold,
But nor heart nor hand hath he to unwrite the scriptures writ of old.
Dead the great chryselephantine God, as dew last evening shed:
Dust of earth or foam of ocean is the symbol of his head:
Earth and ocean shall be shadows when Prometheus shall be dead.

Fame around her warriors living rang through Greece and lightened,   **[Strophe 2.**
Moving equal with their stature, stately with their strength:
Thebes and Lacedæmon at their breathing presence brightened,
Sense or sound of them filled all the live land's breadth and length.
All the lesser tribes put on the pure Athenian fashion,
One Hellenic heart was from the mountains to the sea:
Sparta's bitter self grew sweet with high half-human passion,
And her dry thorns flushed aflower in strait Thermopylæ.
Fruitless yet the flowers had fallen, and all the deeds died fruitless,
Save that tongues of after men, the children of her peace,
Took the tale up of her glories, transient else and rootless,
And in ears and hearts of all men left the praise of Greece.
Fair the war-time was when still, as beacon answering beacon,
Sea to land flashed fight, and thundered note of wrath or cheer;
But the strength of noonday night hath power to waste and weaken,
Nor may light be passed from hand to hand of year to year
If the dying deed be saved not, ere it die for ever,
By the hands and lips of men more wise than years are strong;
If the soul of man take heed not that the deed die never,

Clothed about with purple and gold of story, crowned with song.
Still the burning heart of boy and man alike rejoices,
Hearing words which made it seem of old for all who sang
That their heaven of heavens waxed happier when from free men's voices
Well-beloved Harmodius and Aristogeiton rang.
Never fell such fragrance from the flower-month's rose-red kirtle
As from chaplets on the bright friends' brows who slew their lord:
Greener grew the leaf and balmier blew the flower of myrtle
When its blossom sheathed the sheer tyrannicidal sword.
None so glorious garland crowned the feast Panathenæan
As this wreath too frail to fetter fast the Cyprian dove:
None so fiery song sprang sunwards annual as the pæan
Praising perfect love of friends and perfect country's love.

Higher than highest of all those heavens wherefrom the starry   [Antistrophe 2.
Song of Homer shone above the rolling fight,
Gleams like spring's green bloom on boughs all gaunt and gnarry
Soft live splendour as of flowers of foam in flight,
Glows a glory of mild-winged maidens upward mounting
Sheer through air made shrill with strokes of smooth swift wings
Round the rocks beyond foot's reach, past eyesight's counting,
Up the cleft where iron wind of winter rings
Round a God fast clenched in iron jaws of fetters,
Him who culled for man the fruitful flower of fire,
Bared the darkling scriptures writ in dazzling letters,
Taught the truth of dreams deceiving men's desire,
Gave their water-wandering chariot-seats of ocean
Wings, and bade the rage of war-steeds champ the rein,
Showed the symbols of the wild birds' wheeling motion,
Waged for man's sake war with God and all his train.
Earth, whose name was also Righteousness, a mother
Many-named and single-natured, gave him breath
Whence God's wrath could wring but this word and none other—
He may smite me, yet he shall not do to death.
Him the tongue that sang triumphant while tormented
Sang as loud the sevenfold storm that roared erewhile
Round the towers of Thebes till wrath might rest contented:
Sang the flight from smooth soft-sanded banks of Nile,
When like mateless doves that fly from snare or tether
Came the suppliants landwards trembling as they trod,
And the prayer took wing from all their tongues together—
King of kings, most holy of holies, blessed God.
But what mouth may chant again, what heart may know it,
All the rapture that all hearts of men put on
When of Salamis the time-transcending poet
Sang, whose hand had chased the Mede at Marathon?

Darker dawned the song with stormier wings above the watch-fire spread   [Epode 2.

Whence from Ida toward the hill of Hermes leapt the light that said
Troy was fallen, a torch funereal for the king's triumphal head.
Dire indeed the birth of Leda's womb that had God's self to sire
Bloomed, a flower of love that stung the soul with fangs that gnaw like fire:
But the twin-born human-fathered sister-flower bore fruit more dire.
Scarce the cry that called on airy heaven and all swift winds on wing,
Wells of river-heads, and countless laugh of waves past reckoning,
Earth which brought forth all, and the orbèd sun that looks on everything,
Scarce that cry fills yet men's hearts more full of heart-devouring dread
Than the murderous word said mocking, how the child whose blood he shed
Might clasp fast and kiss her father where the dead salute the dead.
But the latter note of anguish from the lips that mocked her lord,
When her son's hand bared against the breast that suckled him his sword,
How might man endure, O Æschylus, to hear it and record?
How might man endure, being mortal yet, O thou most highest, to hear?
How record, being born of woman? Surely not thy Furies near,
Surely this beheld, this only, blasted hearts to death with fear.
Not the hissing hair, nor flakes of blood that oozed from eyes of fire,
Nor the snort of savage sleep that snuffed the hungering heart's desire
Where the hunted prey found hardly space and harbour to respire;
She whose likeness called them—"Sleep ye, ho? what need of you that sleep?"
(Ah, what need indeed, where she was, of all shapes that night may keep
Hidden dark as death and deeper than men's dreams of hell are deep?)
She the murderess of her husband, she the huntress of her son,
More than ye was she, the shadow that no God withstands but one,
Wisdom equal-eyed and stronger and more splendid than the sun.
Yea, no God may stand betwixt us and the shadows of our deeds,
Nor the light of dreams that lighten darkness, nor the prayer that pleads,
But the wisdom equal-souled with heaven, the light alone that leads.
Light whose law bids home those childless children of eternal night,
Soothed and reconciled and mastered and transmuted in men's sight
Who behold their own souls, clothed with darkness once, now clothed with light.
King of kings and father crowned of all our fathers crowned of yore,
Lord of all the lords of song, whose head all heads bow down before,
Glory be to thee from all thy sons in all tongues evermore.

Rose and vine and olive and deep ivy-bloom entwining   [Strophe 3.
Close the goodliest grave that e'er they closeliest might entwine
Keep the wind from wasting and the sun from too strong shining
Where the sound and light of sweetest songs still float and shine.
Here the music seems to illume the shade, the light to whisper
Song, the flowers to put not odours only forth, but words
Sweeter far than fragrance: here the wandering wreaths twine crisper
Far, and louder far exults the note of all wild birds.
Thoughts that change us, joys that crown and sorrows that enthrone us,
Passions that enrobe us with a clearer air than ours,
Move and breathe as living things beheld round white Colonus,
Audibler than melodies and visibler than flowers.

Love, in fight unconquered, Love, with spoils of great men laden,
Never sang so sweet from throat of woman or of dove:
Love, whose bed by night is in the soft cheeks of a maiden,
And his march is over seas, and low roofs lack not Love;
Nor may one of all that live, ephemeral or eternal,
Fly nor hide from Love; but whoso clasps him fast goes mad.
Never since the first-born year with flowers first-born grew vernal
Such a song made listening hearts of lovers glad or sad.
Never sounded note so radiant at the rayless portal
Opening wide on the all-concealing lowland of the dead
As the music mingling, when her doomsday marked her mortal,
From her own and old men's voices round the bride's way shed,
Round the grave her bride-house, hewn for endless habitation,
Where, shut out from sunshine, with no bridegroom by, she slept;
But beloved of all her dark and fateful generation,
But with all time's tears and praise besprinkled and bewept:
Well-beloved of outcast father and self-slaughtered mother,
Born, yet unpolluted, of their blind incestuous bed;
Best-beloved of him for whose dead sake she died, her brother,
Hallowing by her own life's gift her own born brother's head;

Not with wine or oil nor any less libation   [Antistrophe 3.
Hallowed, nor made sweet with humbler perfume's breath;
Not with only these redeemed from desecration,
But with blood and spirit of life poured forth to death;
Blood unspotted, spirit unsullied, life devoted,
Sister too supreme to make the bride's hope good,
Daughter too divine as woman to be noted,
Spouse of only death in mateless maidenhood.
Yea, in her was all the prayer fulfilled, the saying
All accomplished—Would that fate would let me wear
Hallowed innocence of words and all deeds, weighing
Well the laws thereof, begot on holier air,
Far on high sublimely stablished, whereof only
Heaven is father; nor did birth of mortal mould
Bring them forth, nor shall oblivion lull to lonely
Slumber. Great in these is God, and grows not old.
Therefore even that inner darkness where she perished
Surely seems as holy and lovely, seen aright,
As desirable and as dearly to be cherished,
As the haunt closed in with laurels from the light,
Deep inwound with olive and wild vine inwoven,
Where a godhead known and unknown makes men pale,
But the darkness of the twilight noon is cloven
Still with shrill sweet moan of many a nightingale.
Closer clustering there they make sweet noise together,
Where the fearful gods look gentler than our fear,
And the grove thronged through with birds of holiest feather

Grows nor pale nor dumb with sense of dark things near.
There her father, called upon with signs of wonder,
Passed with tenderest words away by ways unknown,
Not by sea-storm stricken down, nor touched of thunder,
To the dark benign deep underworld, alone.

Third of three that ruled in Athens, kings with sceptral song for staff,   [Epode 3.
Gladdest heart that God gave ever milk and wine of thought to quaff,
Clearest eye that lightened ever to the broad lip's lordliest laugh,
Praise be thine as theirs whose tragic brows the loftier leaf engirds
For the live and lyric lightning of thy honey-hearted words,
Soft like sunny dewy wings of clouds and bright as crying of birds;
Full of all sweet rays and notes that make of earth and air and sea
One great light and sound of laughter from one great God's heart, to be
Sign and semblance of the gladness of man's life where men breathe free.
With no Loxian sound obscure God uttered once, and all time heard,
All the soul of Athens, all the soul of England, in that word:
Rome arose the second child of freedom: northward rose the third.
Ere her Boreal dawn came kindling seas afoam and fields of snow,
Yet again, while Europe groaned and grovelled, shone like suns aglow
Doria splendid over Genoa, Venice bright with Dandolo.
Dead was Hellas, but Ausonia by the light of dead men's deeds
Rose and walked awhile alive, though mocked as whom the fen-fire leads
By the creed-wrought faith of faithless souls that mock their doubts with creeds.
Dead are these, and man is risen again: and haply now the three
Yet coequal and triune may stand in story, marked as free
By the token of the washing of the waters of the sea.
Athens first of all earth's kindred many-tongued and many-kinned
Had the sea to friend and comfort, and for kinsman had the wind:
She that bare Columbus next: then she that made her spoil of Ind.
She that hears not what man's rage but only what the sea-wind saith:
She that turned Spain's ships to cloud-wrack at the blasting of her breath,
By her strengths of strong-souled children and of strong winds done to death.
North and south the Great King's galleons went in Persian wise: and here
She, with Æschylean music on her lips that laughed back fear,
In the face of Time's grey godhead shook the splendour of her spear.
Fair as Athens then with foot upon her foeman's front, and strong
Even as Athens for redemption of the world from sovereign wrong,
Like as Athens crowned she stood before the sun with crowning song.
All the world is theirs with whom is freedom: first of all the free,
Blest are they whom song has crowned and clothed with blessing: these as we,
These alone have part in spirit with the sun that crowns the sea.

April 1881.

THE STATUE OF VICTOR HUGO

I

Since in Athens God stood plain for adoration,
Since the sun beheld his likeness reared in stone,
Since the bronze or gold of human consecration
Gave to Greece her guardian's form and feature shown,
Never hand of sculptor, never heart of nation,
Found so glorious aim in all these ages flown
As is theirs who rear for all time's acclamation
Here the likeness of our mightiest and their own.

II

Theirs and ours and all men's living who behold him
Crowned with garlands multiform and manifold;
Praise and thanksgiving of all mankind enfold him
Who for all men casts abroad his gifts of gold.
With the gods of song have all men's tongues enrolled him,
With the helpful gods have all men's hearts enrolled:
Ours he is who love him, ours whose hearts' hearts hold him
Fast as his the trust that hearts like his may hold.

III

He, the heart most high, the spirit on earth most blameless,
Takes in charge all spirits, holds all hearts in trust:
As the sea-wind's on the sea his ways are tameless,
As the laws that steer the world his works are just.
All most noble feel him nobler, all most shameless
Feel his wrath and scorn make pale their pride and lust:
All most poor and lowliest, all whose wrongs were nameless,
Feel his word of comfort raise them from the dust.

IV

Pride of place and lust of empire bloody-fruited
Knew the blasting of his breath on leaf and fruit:
Now the hand that smote the death-tree now disrooted
Plants the refuge-tree that has man's hope for root.
Ah, but we by whom his darkness was saluted,
How shall now all we that see his day salute?
How should love not seem by love's own speech confuted,
Song before the sovereign singer not be mute?

V

With what worship, by what blessing, in what measure,
May we sing of him, salute him, or adore,
With what hymn for praise, what thanksgiving for pleasure,
Who had given us more than heaven, and gives us more?
Heaven's whole treasury, filled up full with night's whole treasure,
Holds not so divine or deep a starry store
As the soul supreme that deals forth worlds at leisure
Clothed with light and darkness, dense with flower and ore.

VI

Song had touched the bourn: fresh verses overflow it,
Loud and radiant, waves on waves on waves that throng;
Still the tide grows, and the sea-mark still below it
Sinks and shifts and rises, changed and swept along.
Rose it like a rock? the waters overthrow it,
And another stands beyond them sheer and strong:
Goal by goal pays down its prize, and yields its poet
Tribute claimed of triumph, palm achieved of song.

VII

Since his hand that holds the keys of fear and wonder
Opened on the high priest's dreaming eyes a door
Whence the lights of heaven and hell above and under
Shone, and smote the face that men bow down before,
Thrice again one singer's note had cloven in sunder
Night, who blows again not one blast now but four,
And the fourfold heaven is kindled with his thunder,
And the stars about his forehead are fourscore.

VIII

From the deep soul's depths where alway love abounded
First had risen a song with healing on its wings
Whence the dews of mercy raining balms unbounded
Shed their last compassion even on sceptred things.[1]
Even on heads that like a curse the crown surrounded
Fell his crowning pity, soft as cleansing springs;
And the sweet last note his wrath relenting sounded
Bade men's hearts be melted not for slaves but kings.

IX

Next, that faith might strengthen fear and love embolden,
On the creeds of priests a scourge of sunbeams fell:
And its flash made bare the deeps of heaven, beholden
Not of men that cry, Lord, Lord, from church or cell.[2]
Hope as young as dawn from night obscure and olden
Rose again, such power abides in truth's one spell:
Night, if dawn it be that touches her, grows golden;
Tears, if such as angels weep, extinguish hell.

X

Through the blind loud mills of barren blear-eyed learning
Where in dust and darkness children's foreheads bow,
While men's labour, vain as wind or water turning
Wheels and sails of dreams, makes life a leafless bough,
Fell the light of scorn and pity touched with yearning,
Next, from words that shone as heaven's own kindling brow.[3]
Stars were these as watch-fires on the world's waste burning,
Stars that fade not in the fourfold sunrise now.[4]

XI

Now the voice that faints not till all wrongs be wroken
Sounds as might the sun's song from the morning's breast,
All the seals of silence sealed of night are broken,
All the winds that bear the fourfold word are blest.
All the keen fierce east flames forth one fiery token;
All the north is loud with life that knows not rest,
All the south with song as though the stars had spoken;
All the judgment-fire of sunset scathes the west.

XII

Sound of pæan, roll of chanted panegyric,
Though by Pindar's mouth song's trumpet spake forth praise,
March of warrior songs in Pythian mood or Pyrrhic,
Though the blast were blown by lips of ancient days,

Ring not clearer than the clarion of satiric
Song whose breath sweeps bare the plague-infected ways
Till the world be pure as heaven is for the lyric
Sun to rise up clothed with radiant sounds as rays.

XIII

Clear across the cloud-rack fluctuant and erratic
As the strong star smiles that lets no mourner mourn,
Hymned alike from lips of Lesbian choirs or Attic
Once at evensong and morning newly born,
Clear and sure above the changes of dramatic
Tide and current, soft with love and keen with scorn,
Smiles the strong sweet soul of maidenhood, ecstatic
And inviolate as the red glad mouth of morn.

XIV

Pure and passionate as dawn, whose apparition
Thrills with fire from heaven the wheels of hours that whirl,
Rose and passed her radiance in serene transition
From his eyes who sought a grain and found a pearl.
But the food by cunning hope for vain fruition
Lightly stolen away from keeping of a churl
Left the bitterness of death and hope's perdition
On the lip that scorn was wont for shame to curl.[5]

XV

Over waves that darken round the wave-worn rover
Rang his clarion higher than winds cried round the ship,
Rose a pageant of set suns and storms blown over,
Hands that held life's guerdons fast or let them slip.
But no tongue may tell, no thanksgiving discover,
Half the heaven of blessing, soft with clouds that drip,
Keen with beams that kindle, dear as love to lover,
Opening by the spell's strength on his lyric lip.

XVI

By that spell the soul transfigured and dilated
Puts forth wings that widen, breathes a brightening air,
Feeds on light and drinks of music, whence elated
All her sense grows godlike, seeing all depths made bare,
All the mists wherein before she sat belated
Shrink, till now the sunlight knows not if they were;
All this earth transformed is Eden recreated,
With the breath of heaven remurmuring in her hair.

XVII

Sweeter far than aught of sweet that April nurses
Deep in dew-dropt woodland folded fast and furled
Breathes the fragrant song whose burning dawn disperses
Darkness, like the surge of armies backward hurled,
Even as though the touch of spring's own hand, that pierces
Earth with life's delight, had hidden in the impearled
Golden bells and buds and petals of his verses
All the breath of all the flowers in all the world.

XVIII

But the soul therein, the light that our souls follow,
Fires and fills the song with more of prophet's pride,
More of life than all the gulfs of death may swallow,
More of flame than all the might of night may hide.
Though the whole dark age were loud and void and hollow,
Strength of trust were here, and help for all souls tried,
And a token from the flight of that strange swallow[6]
Whose migration still is toward the wintry side.

XIX

Never came such token for divine solution
From the oraculous live darkness whence of yore
Ancient faith sought word of help and retribution,
Truth to lighten doubt, a sign to go before.
Never so baptismal waters of ablution
Bathed the brows of exile on so stern a shore,
Where the lightnings of the sea of revolution
Flashed across them ere its thunders yet might roar.

XX

By the lightning's light of present revelation
Shown, with epic thunder as from skies that frown,
Clothed in darkness as of darkling expiation,
Rose a vision of dead, stars and suns gone down,
Whence of old fierce fire devoured the star-struck nation,
Till its wrath and woe lit red the raging town,
Now made glorious with his statue's crowning station,
Where may never gleam again a viler crown.

King, with time for throne and all the years for pages,
He shall reign though all thrones else be overhurled,
Served of souls that have his living words for wages,
Crowned of heaven each dawn that leaves his brows impearled;
Girt about with robes unrent of storm that rages,
Robes not wrought with hands, from no loom's weft unfurled;
All the praise of all earth's tongues in all earth's ages,
All the love of all men's hearts in all the world.

Yet what hand shall carve the soul or cast the spirit,
Mould the face of fame, bid glory's feature glow?
Who bequeath for eyes of ages hence to inherit
Him, the Master, whom love knows not if it know?
Scarcely perfect praise of men man's work might merit,
Scarcely bid such aim to perfect stature grow,
Were his hand the hand of Phidias who shall rear it,
And his soul the very soul of Angelo.

Michael, awful angel of the world's last session,
Once on earth, like him, with fire of suffering tried,
Thine it were, if man's it were, without transgression,
Thine alone, to take this toil upon thy pride.
Thine, whose heart was great against the world's oppression,
Even as his whose word is lamp and staff and guide:
Advocate for man, untired of intercession,
Pleads his voice for slaves whose lords his voice defied.

Earth, with all the kings and thralls on earth, below it,
Heaven alone, with all the worlds in heaven, above,
Let his likeness rise for suns and stars to know it,
High for men to worship, plain for men to love:
Brow that braved the tides which fain would overflow it,
Lip that gave the challenge, hand that flung the glove;
Comforter and prophet, Paraclete and poet,
Soul whose emblems are an eagle and a dove.

Sun, that hast not seen a loftier head wax hoary,
Earth, which hast not shown the sun a nobler birth,
Time, that hast not on thy scroll defiled and gory
One man's name writ brighter in its whole wide girth,
Witness, till the final years fulfil their story,
Till the stars break off the music of their mirth,
What among the sons of men was this man's glory,
What the vesture of his soul revealed on earth.

FOOTNOTES:
[1] *La Pitié Suprême. 1879.*
[2] *Religions et Religion. 1880.*
[3] *L'Ane. 1880.*
[4] *Les Quatre Vents de l'Esprit. I. Le Livre satirique. II. Le Livre dramatique. III. Le Livre lyrique. IV. Le Livre épique. 1881.*
[5] *Les Deux Trouvailles de Gallus. I. Margarita, comédie. II. Esca, drame.*
[6]
Je suis une hirondelle étrange, car j'émigre
Du côté de l'hiver.
Le Livre Lyrique, liii.

EUTHANATOS

IN MEMORY OF MRS. THELLUSSON

Forth of our ways and woes,
Forth of the winds and snows,
A white soul soaring goes,
Winged like a dove:
So sweet, so pure, so clear,
So heavenly tempered here,
Love need not hope or fear her changed above:

Ere dawned her day to die,
So heavenly, that on high
Change could not glorify
Nor death refine her:
Pure gold of perfect love,
On earth like heaven's own dove,
She cannot wear, above, a smile diviner.

Her voice in heaven's own quire
Can sound no heavenlier lyre
Than here: no purer fire
Her soul can soar:
No sweeter stars her eyes
In unimagined skies
Beyond our sight can rise than here before.

Hardly long years had shed
Their shadows on her head:
Hardly we think her dead,
Who hardly thought her
Old: hardly can believe
The grief our hearts receive
And wonder while they grieve, as wrong were wrought her.

But though strong grief be strong
No word or thought of wrong
May stain the trembling song,
Wring the bruised heart,
That sounds or sighs its faint
Low note of love, nor taint
Grief for so sweet a saint, when such depart.

A saint whose perfect soul,
With perfect love for goal,
Faith hardly might control,
Creeds might not harden:
A flower more splendid far
Than the most radiant star
Seen here of all that are in God's own garden.

Surely the stars we see
Rise and relapse as we,
And change and set, may be
But shadows too:
But spirits that man's lot
Could neither mar nor spot
Like these false lights are not, being heavenly true.

Not like these dying lights
Of worlds whose glory smites
The passage of the nights
Through heaven's blind prison:
Not like their souls who see,
If thought fly far and free,
No heavenlier heaven to be for souls rerisen.

A soul wherein love shone
Even like the sun, alone,
With fervour of its own
And splendour fed,
Made by no creeds less kind
Toward souls by none confined,
Could Death's self quench or blind, Love's self were dead.

February 4, 1881.

FIRST AND LAST

Upon the borderlands of being,
Where life draws hardly breath
Between the lights and shadows fleeing
Fast as a word one saith,
Two flowers rejoice our eyesight, seeing
The dawns of birth and death.

Behind the babe his dawn is lying
Half risen with notes of mirth
From all the winds about it flying
Through new-born heaven and earth:
Before bright age his day for dying
Dawns equal-eyed with birth.

Equal the dews of even and dawn,
Equal the sun's eye seen
A hand's breadth risen and half withdrawn:
But no bright hour between
Brings aught so bright by stream or lawn
To noonday growths of green.

Which flower of life may smell the sweeter
To love's insensual sense,
Which fragrance move with offering meeter
His soothed omnipotence,
Being chosen as fairer or as fleeter,
Borne hither or borne hence,
Love's foiled omniscience knows not: this
Were more than all he knows
With all his lore of bale and bliss,
The choice of rose and rose,
One red as lips that touch with his,
One white as moonlit snows.

No hope is half so sweet and good,
No dream of saint or sage
So fair as these are: no dark mood
But these might best assuage;
The sweet red rose of babyhood,
The white sweet rose of age.

LINES ON THE DEATH OF EDWARD JOHN TRELAWNY

Last high star of the years whose thunder
Still men's listening remembrance hears,
Last light left of our fathers' years,
Watched with honour and hailed with wonder
Thee too then have the years borne under,
Thou too then hast regained thy peers.

Wings that warred with the winds of morning,
Storm-winds rocking the red great dawn,
Close at last, and a film is drawn
Over the eyes of the storm-bird, scorning
Now no longer the loud wind's warning,
Waves that threaten or waves that fawn.

Peers were none of thee left us living,
Peers of theirs we shall see no more.
Eight years over the full fourscore
Knew thee: now shalt thou sleep, forgiving
All griefs past of the wild world's giving,
Moored at last on the stormless shore.

Worldwide liberty's lifelong lover,
Lover no less of the strength of song,
Sea-king, swordsman, hater of wrong,
Over thy dust that the dust shall cover
Comes my song as a bird to hover,
Borne of its will as of wings along.

Cherished of thee were this brief song's brothers
Now that follows them, cherishing thee.
Over the tides and the tideless sea
Soft as a smile of the earth our mother's
Flies it faster than all those others,
First of the troop at thy tomb to be.

Memories of Greece and the mountain's hollow
Guarded alone of thy loyal sword

Hold thy name for our hearts in ward:
Yet more fain are our hearts to follow
One way now with the southward swallow
Back to the grave of the man their lord.

Heart of hearts, art thou moved not, hearing
Surely, if hearts of the dead may hear,
Whose true heart it is now draws near?
Surely the sense of it thrills thee, cheering
Darkness and death with the news now nearing—
Shelley, Trelawny rejoins thee here.

ADIEUX À MARIE STUART

I

Queen, for whose house my fathers fought,
With hopes that rose and fell,
Red star of boyhood's fiery thought,
Farewell.

They gave their lives, and I, my queen,
Have given you of my life,
Seeing your brave star burn high between
Men's strife.

The strife that lightened round their spears
Long since fell still: so long
Hardly may hope to last in years
My song.

But still through strife of time and thought
Your light on me too fell:
Queen, in whose name we sang or fought,
Farewell.

II

There beats no heart on either border
Where through the north blasts blow
But keeps your memory as a warder
His beacon-fire aglow.

Long since it fired with love and wonder
Mine, for whose April age

Blithe midsummer made banquet under
The shade of Hermitage.

Soft sang the burn's blithe notes, that gather
Strength to ring true:
And air and trees and sun and heather
Remembered you.

Old border ghosts of fight or fairy
Or love or teen,
These they forgot, remembering Mary
The Queen.

III

Queen once of Scots and ever of ours
Whose sires brought forth for you
Their lives to strew your way like flowers.
Adieu.

Dead is full many a dead man's name
Who died for you this long
Time past: shall this too fare the same,
My song?

But surely, though it die or live,
Your face was worth
All that a man may think to give
On earth.

No darkness cast of years between
Can darken you:
Man's love will never bid my queen
Adieu.

IV

Love hangs like light about your name
As music round the shell:
No heart can take of you a tame
Farewell.

Yet, when your very face was seen,
Ill gifts were yours for giving:
Love gat strange guerdons of my queen
When living.

O diamond heart unflawed and clear,
The whole world's crowning jewel!
Was ever heart so deadly dear
So cruel?

Yet none for you of all that bled
Grudged once one drop that fell:
Not one to life reluctant said
Farewell.

V

Strange love they have given you, love disloyal,
Who mock with praise your name,
To leave a head so rare and royal
Too low for praise or blame.

You could not love nor hate, they tell us,
You had nor sense nor sting:
In God's name, then, what plague befell us
To fight for such a thing?

"Some faults the gods will give," to fetter
Man's highest intent:
But surely you were something better
Than innocent!

No maid that strays with steps unwary
Through snares unseen,
But one to live and die for; Mary,
The Queen.

VI

Forgive them all their praise, who blot
Your fame with praise of you:
Then love may say, and falter not,
Adieu.

Yet some you hardly would forgive
Who did you much less wrong
Once: but resentment should not live
Too long.

They never saw your lip's bright bow,

Your swordbright eyes,
The bluest of heavenly things below
The skies.

Clear eyes that love's self finds most like
A swordblade's blue,
A swordblade's ever keen to strike,
Adieu.

VII

Though all things breathe or sound of fight
That yet make up your spell,
To bid you were to bid the light
Farewell.

Farewell the song says only, being
A star whose race is run:
Farewell the soul says never, seeing
The sun.

Yet, well-nigh as with flash of tears,
The song must say but so
That took your praise up twenty years
Ago.

More bright than stars or moons that vary,
Sun kindling heaven and hell,
Here, after all these years, Queen Mary,
Farewell.

HERSE

When grace is given us ever to behold
A child some sweet months old,
Love, laying across our lips his finger, saith,
Smiling, with bated breath,
Hush! for the holiest thing that lives is here,
And heaven's own heart how near!
How dare we, that may gaze not on the sun,
Gaze on this verier one?
Heart, hold thy peace; eyes, be cast down for shame;
Lips, breathe not yet its name.
In heaven they know what name to call it; we,
How should we know? For, see!

The adorable sweet living marvellous
Strange light that lightens us
Who gaze, desertless of such glorious grace,
Full in a babe's warm face!
All roses that the morning rears are nought,
All stars not worth a thought,
Set this one star against them, or suppose
As rival this one rose.
What price could pay with earth's whole weight of gold
One least flushed roseleaf's fold
Of all this dimpling store of smiles that shine
From each warm curve and line,
Each charm of flower-sweet flesh, to reillume
The dappled rose-red bloom
Of all its dainty body, honey-sweet
Clenched hands and curled-up feet,
That on the roses of the dawn have trod
As they came down from God,
And keep the flush and colour that the sky
Takes when the sun comes nigh,
And keep the likeness of the smile their grace
Evoked on God's own face
When, seeing this work of his most heavenly mood,
He saw that it was good?
For all its warm sweet body seems one smile,
And mere men's love too vile
To meet it, or with eyes that worship dims
Read o'er the little limbs,
Read all the book of all their beauties o'er,
Rejoice, revere, adore,
Bow down and worship each delight in turn,
Laugh, wonder, yield, and yearn.
But when our trembling kisses dare, yet dread,
Even to draw nigh its head,
And touch, and scarce with touch or breath surprise
Its mild miraculous eyes
Out of their viewless vision—O, what then,
What may be said of men?
What speech may name a new-born child? what word
Earth ever spake or heard?
The best men's tongue that ever glory knew
Called that a drop of dew
Which from the breathing creature's kindly womb
Came forth in blameless bloom.
We have no word, as had those men most high,
To call a baby by.
Rose, ruby, lily, pearl of stormless seas—
A better word than these,

A better sign it was than flower or gem
That love revealed to them:
They knew that whence comes light or quickening flame,
Thence only this thing came,
And only might be likened of our love
To somewhat born above,
Not even to sweetest things dropped else on earth,
Only to dew's own birth.
Nor doubt we but their sense was heavenly true,
Babe, when we gaze on you,
A dew-drop out of heaven whose colours are
More bright than sun or star,
As now, ere watching love dare fear or hope,
Lips, hands, and eyelids ope,
And all your life is mixed with earthly leaven.
O child, what news from heaven?

TWINS

AFFECTIONATELY INSCRIBED TO W. M. R. AND L. R.

April, on whose wings
Ride all gracious things,
Like the star that brings
All things good to man,
Ere his light, that yet
Makes the month shine, set,
And fair May forget
Whence her birth began,

Brings, as heart would choose,
Sound of golden news,
Bright as kindling dews
When the dawn begins;
Tidings clear as mirth,
Sweet as air and earth
Now that hail the birth,
Twice thus blest, of twins.

In the lovely land
Where with hand in hand
Lovers wedded stand
Other joys before
Made your mixed life sweet:
Now, as Time sees meet,
Three glad blossoms greet

Two glad blossoms more.

Fed with sun and dew,
While your joys were new,
First arose and grew
One bright olive-shoot:
Then a fair and fine
Slip of warm-haired pine
Felt the sweet sun shine
On its leaf and fruit.

And it wore for mark
Graven on the dark
Beauty of its bark
That the noblest name
Worn in song of old
By the king whose bold
Hand had fast in hold
All the flower of fame.

Then, with southern skies
Flattered in her eyes,
Which, in lovelier wise
Yet, reflect their blue
Brightened more, being bright
Here with life's delight,
And with love's live light
Glorified anew,

Came, as fair as came
One who bore her name
(She that broke as flame
From the swan-shell white),
Crowned with tender hair
Only, but more fair
Than all queens that were
Themes of oldworld fight,

Of your flowers the third
Bud, or new-fledged bird
In your hearts' nest heard
Murmuring like a dove
Bright as those that drew
Over waves where blew
No loud wind the blue
Heaven-hued car of love.

Not the glorious grace

Even of that one face
Potent to displace
All the towers of Troy
Surely shone more clear
Once with childlike cheer
Than this child's face here
Now with living joy.

After these again
Here in April's train
Breaks the bloom of twain
Blossoms in one birth
For a crown of May
On the front of day
When he takes his way
Over heaven and earth.

Half a heavenly thing
Given from heaven to Spring
By the sun her king,
Half a tender toy,
Seems a child of curl
Yet too soft to twirl;
Seems the flower-sweet girl
By the flower-bright boy.

All the kind gods' grace,
All their love, embrace
Ever either face,
Ever brood above them:
All soft wings of hours
Screen them as with flowers
From all beams and showers:
All life's seasons love them.

When the dews of sleep
Falling lightliest keep
Eyes too close to peep
Forth and laugh off rest,
Joy from face to feet
Fill them, as is meet:
Life to them be sweet
As their mother's breast.

When those dews are dry,
And in day's bright eye
Looking full they lie
Bright as rose and pearl,

All returns of joy
Pure of time's alloy
Bless the rose-red boy,
Guard the rose-white girl.

POSTSCRIPT

Friends, if I could take
Half a note from Blake
Or but one verse make
Of the Conqueror's mine,
Better than my best
Song above your nest
I would sing: the quest
Now seems too divine.

April 28, 1881.

THE SALT OF THE EARTH

If childhood were not in the world,
But only men and women grown;
No baby-locks in tendrils curled,
No baby-blossoms blown;

Though men were stronger, women fairer,
And nearer all delights in reach,
And verse and music uttered rarer
Tones of more godlike speech;

Though the utmost life of life's best hours
Found, as it cannot now find, words;
Though desert sands were sweet as flowers
And flowers could sing like birds,

But children never heard them, never
They felt a child's foot leap and run
This were a drearier star than ever
Yet looked upon the sun.

SEVEN YEARS OLD

I

Seven white roses on one tree,
Seven white loaves of blameless leaven,
Seven white sails on one soft sea,
Seven white swans on one lake's lee,
Seven white flowerlike stars in heaven,
All are types unmeet to be
For a birthday's crown of seven.

II

Not the radiance of the roses,
Not the blessing of the bread,
Not the breeze that ere day grows is
Fresh for sails and swans, and closes
Wings above the sun's grave spread,
When the starshine on the snows is
Sweet as sleep on sorrow shed.

III

Nothing sweetest, nothing best,
Holds so good and sweet a treasure
As the love wherewith once blest
Joy grows holy, grief takes rest,
Life, half tired with hours to measure,
Fills his eyes and lips and breast
With most light and breath of pleasure;

IV

As the rapture unpolluted,
As the passion undefiled,
By whose force all pains heart-rooted
Are transfigured and transmuted,
Recompensed and reconciled,
Through the imperial, undisputed,
Present godhead of a child.

V

Brown bright eyes and fair bright head,
Worth a worthier crown than this is,
Worth a worthier song instead,

Sweet grave wise round mouth, full fed
With the joy of love, whose bliss is
More than mortal wine and bread,
Lips whose words are sweet as kisses,

VI

Little hands so glad of giving,
Little heart so glad of love,
Little soul so glad of living,
While the strong swift hours are weaving
Light with darkness woven above,
Time for mirth and time for grieving,
Plume of raven and plume of dove,

VII

I can give you but a word
Warm with love therein for leaven,
But a song that falls unheard
Yet on ears of sense unstirred
Yet by song so far from heaven,
Whence you came the brightest bird,
Seven years since, of seven times seven.

EIGHT YEARS OLD

I

Sun, whom the faltering snow-cloud fears,
Rise, let the time of year be May,
Speak now the word that April hears,
Let March have all his royal way;
Bid all spring raise in winter's ears
All tunes her children hear or play,
Because the crown of eight glad years
On one bright head is set to-day.

II

What matters cloud or sun to-day
To him who wears the wreath of years
So many, and all like flowers at play

With wind and sunshine, while his ears
Hear only song on every way?
More sweet than spring triumphant hears
Ring through the revel-rout of May
Are these, the notes that winter fears.

III

Strong-hearted winter knows and fears
The music made of love at play,
Or haply loves the tune he hears
From hearts fulfilled with flowering May,
Whose molten music thaws his ears
Late frozen, deaf but yesterday
To sounds of dying and dawning years,
Now quickened on his deathward way.

IV

For deathward now lies winter's way
Down the green vestibule of years
That each year brightens day by day
With flower and shower till hope scarce fears
And fear grows wholly hope of May.
But we—the music in our ears
Made of love's pulses as they play
The heart alone that makes it hears.

V

The heart it is that plays and hears
High salutation of to-day.
Tongue falters, hand shrinks back, song fears
Its own unworthiness to play
Fit music for those eight sweet years,
Or sing their blithe accomplished way.
No song quite worth a young child's ears
Broke ever even from birds in May.

VI

There beats not in the heart of May,
When summer hopes and springtide fears,
There falls not from the height of day,

When sunlight speaks and silence hears,
So sweet a psalm as children play
And sing, each hour of all their years,
Each moment of their lovely way,
And know not how it thrills our ears.

VII

Ah child, what are we, that our ears
Should hear you singing on your way,
Should have this happiness? The years
Whose hurrying wings about us play
Are not like yours, whose flower-time fears
Nought worse than sunlit showers in May,
Being sinless as the spring, that hears
Her own heart praise her every day.

VIII

Yet we too triumph in the day
That bare, to entrance our eyes and ears,
To lighten daylight, and to play
Such notes as darkness knows and fears,
The child whose face illumes our way,
Whose voice lifts up the heart that hears,
Whose hand is as the hand of May
To bring us flowers from eight full years.

February 4, 1882.

COMPARISONS

Child, when they say that others
Have been or are like you,
Babes fit to be your brothers,
Sweet human drops of dew,
Bright fruit of mortal mothers,
What should one say or do?

We know the thought is treason,
We feel the dream absurd;
A claim rebuked of reason,
That withers at a word:
For never shone the season

That bore so blithe a bird.

Some smiles may seem as merry,
Some glances gleam as wise,
From lips as like a cherry
And scarce less gracious eyes;
Eyes browner than a berry,
Lips red as morning's rise.

But never yet rang laughter
So sweet in gladdened ears
Through wall and floor and rafter
As all this household hears
And rings response thereafter
Till cloudiest weather clears.

When those your chosen of all men,
Whose honey never cloys,
Two lights whose smiles enthrall men,
Were called at your age boys,
Those mighty men, while small men,
Could make no merrier noise.

Our Shakespeare, surely, daffed not
More lightly pain aside
From radiant lips that quaffed not
Of forethought's tragic tide:
Our Dickens, doubtless, laughed not
More loud with life's first pride.

The dawn were not more cheerless
With neither light nor dew
Than we without the fearless
Clear laugh that thrills us through:
If ever child stood peerless,
Love knows that child is you.

WHAT IS DEATH?

Looking on a page where stood
Graven of old on old-world wood
Death, and by the grave's edge grim,
Pale, the young man facing him,
Asked my well-beloved of me
Once what strange thing; this might be,
Gaunt and great of limb.

Death, I told him: and, surprise
Deepening more his wildwood eyes
(Like some sweet fleet thing's whose breath
Speaks all spring though nought it saith),
Up he turned his rosebright face
Glorious with its seven years' grace,
Asking—What is death?

A CHILD'S PITY

No sweeter thing than children's ways and wiles,
Surely, we say, can gladden eyes and ears:
Yet sometime sweeter than their words or smiles
Are even their tears.

To one for once a piteous tale was read,
How, when the murderous mother crocodile
Was slain, her fierce brood famished, and lay dead,
Starved, by the Nile.

In vast green reed-beds on the vast grey slime
Those monsters motherless and helpless lay,
Perishing only for the parent's crime
Whose seed were they.

Hours after, toward the dusk, our blithe small bird
Of Paradise, who has our hearts in keeping,
Was heard or seen, but hardly seen or heard,
For pity weeping.

He was so sorry, sitting still apart,
For the poor little crocodiles, he said.
Six years had given him, for an angel's heart,
A child's instead.

Feigned tears the false beasts shed for murderous ends,
We know from travellers' tales of crocodiles:
But these tears wept upon them of my friend's
Outshine his smiles.

What heavenliest angels of what heavenly city
Could match the heavenly heart in children here?
The heart that hallowing all things with its pity
Casts out all fear?

So lovely, so divine, so dear their laughter
Seems to us, we know not what could be more dear:
But lovelier yet we see the sign thereafter
Of such a tear.

With sense of love half laughing and half weeping
We met your tears, our small sweet-spirited friend:
Let your love have us in its heavenly keeping
To life's last end.

A CHILD'S LAUGHTER

All the bells of heaven may ring,
All the birds of heaven may sing,
All the wells on earth may spring,
All the winds on earth may bring
All sweet sounds together;
Sweeter far than all things heard,
Hand of harper, tone of bird,
Sound of woods at sundawn stirred,
Welling water's winsome word,
Wind in warm wan weather,

One thing yet there is, that none
Hearing ere its chime be done
Knows not well the sweetest one
Heard of man beneath the sun,
Hoped in heaven hereafter;
Soft and strong and loud and light,
Very sound of very light
Heard from morning's rosiest height,
When the soul of all delight
Fills a child's clear laughter.

Golden bells of welcome rolled
Never forth such notes, nor told
Hours so blithe in tones so bold,
As the radiant mouth of gold
Here that rings forth heaven.
If the golden-crested wren
Were a nightingale—why, then,
Something seen and heard of men
Might be half as sweet as when
Laughs a child of seven.

A CHILD'S THANKS

How low soe'er men rank us,
How high soe'er we win,
The children far above us
Dwell, and they deign to love us,
With lovelier love than ours,
And smiles more sweet than flowers;
As though the sun should thank us
For letting light come in.

With too divine complaisance,
Whose grace misleads them thus,
Being gods, in heavenly blindness
They call our worship kindness,
Our pebble-gift a gem:
They think us good to them,
Whose glance, whose breath, whose presence,
Are gifts too good for us.

The poet high and hoary
Of meres that mountains bind
Felt his great heart more often
Yearn, and its proud strength soften
From stern to tenderer mood,
At thought of gratitude
Shown than of song or story
He heard of hearts unkind.

But with what words for token
And what adoring tears
Of reverence risen to passion,
In what glad prostrate fashion
Of spirit and soul subdued,
May man show gratitude
For thanks of children spoken
That hover in his ears?

The angels laugh, your brothers,
Child, hearing you thank me,
With eyes whence night grows sunny,
And touch of lips like honey,
And words like honey-dew:
But how shall I thank you?
For gifts above all others
What guerdon-gift may be?

What wealth of words caressing,
What choice of songs found best,
Would seem not as derision,
Found vain beside the vision
And glory from above
Shown in a child's heart's love?
His part in life is blessing;
Ours, only to be blest.

A CHILD'S BATTLES

pyx aretan heurôn.—PINDAR.

Praise of the knights of old
May sleep: their tale is told,
And no man cares:
The praise which fires our lips is
A knight's whose fame eclipses
All of theirs.

The ruddiest light in heaven
Blazed as his birth-star seven
Long years ago:
All glory crown that old year
Which brought our stout small soldier
With the snow!

Each baby born has one
Star, for his friends a sun,
The first of stars:
And we, the more we scan it,
The more grow sure your planet,
Child, was Mars.

For each one flower, perchance,
Blooms as his cognizance:
The snowdrop chill,
The violet unbeholden,
For some: for you the golden
Daffodil.

Erect, a fighting flower,
It breasts the breeziest hour
That ever blew.
And bent or broke things brittle
Or frail, unlike a little

Knight like you.

Its flower is firm and fresh
And stout like sturdiest flesh
Of children: all
The strenuous blast that parches
Spring hurts it not till March is
Near his fall.

If winds that prate and fret
Remark, rebuke, regret,
Lament, or blame
The brave plant's martial passion,
It keeps its own free fashion
All the same.

We that would fain seem wise
Assume grave mouths and eyes
Whose looks reprove
Too much delight in battle:
But your great heart our prattle
Cannot move.

We say, small children should
Be placid, mildly good
And blandly meek:
Whereat the broad smile rushes
Full on your lips, and flushes
All your cheek.

If all the stars that are
Laughed out, and every star
Could here be heard,
Such peals of golden laughter
We should not hear, as after
Such a word.

For all the storm saith, still,
Stout stands the daffodil:
For all we say,
Howe'er he look demurely,
Our martialist will surely
Have his way.

We may not bind with bands
Those large and liberal hands,
Nor stay from fight,
Nor hold them back from giving:

No lean mean laws of living
Bind a knight.

And always here of old
Such gentle hearts and bold
Our land has bred:
How durst her eye rest else on
The glory shed from Nelson
Quick and dead?

Shame were it, if but one
Such once were born her son,
That one to have borne,
And brought him ne'er a brother:
His praise should bring his mother
Shame and scorn.

A child high-souled as he
Whose manhood shook the sea
Smiles haply here:
His face, where love lies basking,
With bright shut mouth seems asking,
What is fear?

The sunshine-coloured fists
Beyond his dimpling wrists
Were never closed
For saving or for sparing—
For only deeds of daring
Predisposed.

Unclenched, the gracious hands
Let slip their gifts like sands
Made rich with ore
That tongues of beggars ravish
From small stout hands so lavish
Of their store.

Sweet hardy kindly hands
Like these were his that stands
With heel on gorge
Seen trampling down the dragon
On sign or flask or flagon,
Sweet Saint George.

Some tournament, perchance,
Of hands that couch no lance,
Might mark this spot

Your lists, if here some pleasant
Small Guenevere were present,
Launcelot.

My brave bright flower, you need
No foolish song, nor heed
It more than spring
The sighs of winter stricken
Dead when your haunts requicken
Here, my king.

Yet O, how hardly may
The wheels of singing stay
That whirl along
Bright paths whence echo raises
The phantom of your praises,
Child, my song!

Beyond all other things
That give my words fleet wings,
Fleet wings and strong,
You set their jesses ringing
Till hardly can I, singing,
Stint my song.

But all things better, friend,
And worse must find an end:
And, right or wrong,
'Tis time, lest rhyme should baffle,
I doubt, to put a snaffle
On my song.

And never may your ear
Aught harsher hear or fear,
Nor wolfish night
Nor dog-toothed winter snarling
Behind your steps, my darling
My delight!

For all the gifts you give
Me, dear, each day you live,
Of thanks above
All thanks that could be spoken
Take not my song in token,
Take my love.

A CHILD'S FUTURE

What will it please you, my darling, hereafter to be?
Fame upon land will you look for, or glory by sea?
Gallant your life will be always, and all of it free.

Free as the wind when the heart of the twilight is stirred
Eastward, and sounds from the springs of the sunrise are heard:
Free—and we know not another as infinite word.

Darkness or twilight or sunlight may compass us round,
Hate may arise up against us, or hope may confound;
Love may forsake us; yet may not the spirit be bound.

Free in oppression of grief as in ardour of joy
Still may the soul be, and each to her strength as a toy:
Free in the glance of the man as the smile of the boy.

Freedom alone is the salt and the spirit that gives
Life, and without her is nothing that verily lives:
Death cannot slay her: she laughs upon death and forgives.

Brightest and hardiest of roses anear and afar
Glitters the blithe little face of you, round as a star:
Liberty bless you and keep you to be as you are.

England and liberty bless you and keep you to be
Worthy the name of their child and the sight of their sea:
Fear not at all; for a slave, if he fears not, is free.

SUNRISE

If the wind and the sunlight of April and August had mingled the past and hereafter
In a single adorable season whose life were a rapture of love and of laughter,
And the blithest of singers were back with a song; if again from his tomb as from prison,
If again from the night or the twilight of ages Aristophanes had arisen,
With the gold-feathered wings of a bird that were also a god upon earth at his shoulders,
And the gold-flowing laugh of the manhood of old at his lips, for a joy to beholders,
He alone unrebuked of presumption were able to set to some adequate measure
The delight of our eyes in the dawn that restores them the sun of their sense and the pleasure.
For the days of the darkness of spirit are over for all of us here, and the season
When desire was a longing, and absence a thorn, and rejoicing a word without reason.
For the roof overhead of the pines is astir with delight as of jubilant voices,
And the floor underfoot of the bracken and heather alive as a heart that rejoices.
For the house that was childless awhile, and the light of it darkened, the pulse of it dwindled,
Rings radiant again with a child's bright feet, with the light of his face is rekindled.

And the ways of the meadows that knew him, the sweep of the down that the sky's belt closes,
Grow gladder at heart than the soft wind made them whose feet were but fragrant with roses,
Though the fall of the year be upon us, who trusted in June and by June were defrauded,
And the summer that brought us not back the desire of our eyes be gone hence unapplauded.
For July came joyless among us, and August went out from us arid and sterile,
And the hope of our hearts, as it seemed, was no more than a flower that the seasons imperil,
And the joy of our hearts, as it seemed, than a thought which regret had not heart to remember,
Till four dark months overpast were atoned for, and summer began in September.
Hark, April again as a bird in the house with a child's voice hither and thither:
See, May in the garden again with a child's face cheering the woods ere they wither.
June laughs in the light of his eyes, and July on the sunbright cheeks of him slumbers,
And August glows in a smile more sweet than the cadence of gold-mouthed numbers.
In the morning the sight of him brightens the sun, and the noon with delight in him flushes,
And the silence of nightfall is music about him as soft as the sleep that it hushes.
We awake with a sense of a sunrise that is not a gift of the sundawn's giving,
And a voice that salutes us is sweeter than all sounds else in the world of the living,
And a presence that warms us is brighter than all in the world of our visions beholden,
Though the dreams of our sleep were as those that the light of a world without grief makes golden.
For the best that the best of us ever devised as a likeness of heaven and its glory,
What was it of old, or what is it and will be for ever, in song or in story,
Or in shape or in colour of carven or painted resemblance, adored of all ages,
But a vision recorded of children alive in the pictures of old or the pages?
Where children are not, heaven is not, and heaven if they come not again shall be never:
But the face and the voice of a child are assurance of heaven and its promise for ever.

Algernon Charles Swinburne – A Short Biography

Algernon Charles Swinburne was born at 7 Chester Street, Grosvenor Place, in London, on April 5th, 1837. He was the eldest of six children born to Captain Charles Henry Swinburne and Lady Jane Henrietta, daughter of the 3rd Earl of Ashburnham, a wealthy Northumbrian family.

Swinburne spent his early years at East Dene in Bonchurch, on the Isle of Wight. As a child, Swinburne was nervous and frail, but also imbued with a nervous energy and fearlessness almost to the point of recklessness.

He was schooled at Eton College from 1849 to 1853. It was here that he first began to write poetry. He excelled at languages and whilst still at Eton won first prizes in both French and Italian.

From Eton he moved to Oxford where he attended at Balliol College from 1856. Here he met friends to whom he became closely attached, among them Dante Gabriel Rossetti, William Morris and Edward Burne-Jones, who in 1857, were painting their Arthurian murals on the walls of the Oxford Union. At Oxford Swinburne was mentored by Benjamin Jowett, the master of Balliol College, who recognised his poetic talent and, intervening on his behalf, tried to keep him from being expelled when he celebrated the Italian patriot Orsini, and his failed attempt on the life of Napoleon III in 1858. Swinburne had to leave the Universcity for a few months due to this but returned in May, 1860 but never received a degree.

Summers were usually spent at Capheaton Hall in Northumberland, the house of his grandfather, Sir John Swinburne, 6th Baronet, who had a famous library and was himself President of the Literary and Philosophical Society in Newcastle upon Tyne.

Swinburne proudly considered himself a native of Northumberland and this is reflected in poems such as the intensely patriotic 'Northumberland' and 'Grace Darling'. He enjoyed riding across the moors and was, it was said, a daring horseman, as he moved 'through honeyed leagues of the northland border', as he remembered the Scottish border in his Recollections.

In the period from 1857 to 1860, Swinburne was one of a number of Pre-Raphaelite's who visited and became part of Lady Pauline Trevelyan's intellectual circle at Wallington Hall, a few miles west of Morpeth in Northumberland.

After leaving college, he moved to London and began his career in earnest as well as becoming a constant visitor to the Rossetti's house. To Rossetti Swinburne was his 'little Northumbrian friend', an affectionate reference to Swinburne's small stature—a mere five foot four. Whatever Swinburne lacked in height he made up for in poetic talent. However, with the burden of such great talent came the unveiling of a dark side that was to cause him pain and would, at times, threaten his very existence with all manner of self-inflicted pains through drink, drugs and sado-machoism.

In 1860 Swinburne published two verse dramas; The Queen Mother and Rosamond but it would not be until 1865 that Swinburne would achieve literary success with Atalanta in Calydon.

In 1861, Swinburne visited Menton on the French Riviera to recover from the effects of yet another period of excess use of alcohol, staying at the Villa Laurenti. From Menton, Swinburne then travelled on to Italy, where he journeyed widely.

After Elizabeth Rossetti's death from suicide in 1862, he and Rossetti moved to Tudor House at 16 Cheyne Walk in Chelsea. The stories that survive from his year with Rossetti are typical Swinburne. In one, Rossetti once had to tell him to keep down the noise — he and a boyfriend had been sliding naked down the bannisters and disturbing Rossetti's painting. He took a sardonic delight in what the critic and biographer, Cecil Lang, calls "Algernonic exaggeration": When people began to talk scathingly about his homosexuality and other sexual proclivities, he circulated a story that he had engaged in pederasty and bestiality with a monkey — and then eaten it. How many of the stories were true and how many invented is unclear. Oscar Wilde called him "a braggart in matters of vice, who had done everything he could to convince his fellow citizens of his homosexuality and bestiality without being in the slightest degree a homosexual or a bestialiser."

In December 1862, Swinburne accompanied Scott and his guests on a trip to Tynemouth. Scott writes in his memoirs that, as they walked by the sea, Swinburne declaimed the as yet unpublished 'Hymn to Proserpine' and 'Laus Veneris' in his lilting intonation, while the waves 'were running the whole length of the long level sands towards Cullercoats and sounding like far-off acclamations'.

Swinburne possessed a curious combination of frail health and strength. He was small and slightly built, but an excellent swimmer and the first to climb Culver Cliff on the Isle of Wight. He had an extremely excitable disposition: people who met him described him as a "demoniac boy" who would go skipping about the room declaiming poetry at the top of his voice. In this as in many things, moderation was not the standard for him. Excess was. Once or twice he had fits, thought to be epileptic, in public; but he made this condition much worse by drinking past excess to unconsciousness. More than once he was delivered to the door in the small of the night, dead drunk. Throughout the 1860s and '70s he rode an alcoholic cycle of dissolution, collapse, drying out at home in the country, then returning to London where he would begin the cycle all over again.

His mania for masochism, particularly flagellation, most probably started in early childhood at Eton and was encouraged by his later friendships with Richard Monckton Milnes (one of Tennyson's fellow Apostles), who introduced him to the works of the Marquis de Sade, and Richard Burton, the Victorian explorer and adventurer. Swinburne was an alcoholic and algolagniac (a desire for sexual gratification through inflicting pain on oneself or others; sadomasochism). He found life difficult, unfulfilling but still his poetic talents pushed to the fore.

Although Swinburne continued to publish some works in periodicals in 1865 he was granted recognition by both public and critics with Atalanta in Calydon written in the style of a classical Greek tragedy.

There followed "Laus Veneris" and Poems and Ballads (1866), with their sexually charged passages, absolutely decadent for polite Victorian society, which were attacked all the more violently as a result. The poems written in homage of Sappho of Lesbos such as "Anactoria" and "Sapphics" were especially savaged. The volume also contained poems such as "The Leper," "Laus Veneris," and "St Dorothy" which evoke both Swinburne's and a general Victorian fascination with the Middle Ages, and are explicitly mediaeval in style, tone and construction. With its publication came instant notoriety. He was now identified with indecent and decadent themes and the precept of art for art's sake.

Swinburne's meeting in 1867 with his long-time hero Mazzini, the Italian patriot living in England in exile, was the beginning of a poetical journey that now became more serious and more engaged with serious thought, initially leading to the political poems in the volume Songs Before Sunrise.

Also in 1867 he was introduced to Adah Isaacs Menken, the American actress, poet and circus rider, whose main fame seemed to be riding naked on a horse (in fact she wore tight nude coloured clothing) for her performance in the melodrama Mazeppa (itself based on a poem by Lord Byron). Although they had a short affair Adah's quote implies that Swinburne was not ready for a relationship that did not involve some self-sabotage; "I can't make him understand that biting's no use."

In 1879, with Swinburne nearly dead from alcoholism and dissolution, his legal advisor Theodore Watts-Dunton took him in, and was gradually successful in getting him to adapt to a healthier lifestyle. Swinburne lived the rest of his life at Watts-Dunton's house. He saw less and less of his old bohemian friends, who thought him a prisoner at The Pines, but his growing deafness also accounts for some of his decreased sociability. By now Swinburne was 42, and was moving from a young man of rebelliousness to a figure of social respectability. It was said of Watts-Dunton that he saved the man and killed the poet.

It is clear that Swinburne had an addictive personality, and clearly incapable of moderation in his pursuit of any chosen vices. This, of course, would both nourish and perhaps sabotage his poetic career. His poetry follows the somewhat clichéd pattern of early flourish and later decline; indeed some of the fresher pieces in the second and third series of Poems and Ballads (published in 1878 and 1889) were actually written during his days at Oxford. Nevertheless, his last collection, A Channel Passage, has some beautiful poems, including "The Lake of Gaube."

He is best remembered as the supreme technician in metre, with a versatility which exceeds even Tennyson's, but which lacks a corresponding emotional range. His obsessions are not widely enough shared; and if he cannot shock us by the strangeness of his desires nor the shrillness of his anti-theistical exclamations, often what remains is not enough to fully engage with the audience.

Swinburne is considered a poet of the decadent school, although he perhaps professed to more vice than he actually indulged in to advertise his deviance. Common gossip of the time reported that he also had a deep crush on the explorer Sir Richard Francis Burton, despite the fact that Swinburne himself abhorred travel. Fact and fiction are easily absorbed by the other so are difficult to untangle even now.

Many critics consider his mastery of vocabulary, rhyme and metre impressive, although he has also been criticised for his florid style and word choices that only fit the rhyme scheme rather than contributing to the meaning of the piece. A. E. Housman, although a critic, had great praise for his rhyming ability: to Swinburne the sonnet was child's play: the task of providing four rhymes was not hard enough, and he wrote long poems in which each stanza required eight or ten rhymes, and wrote them so that he never seemed to be saying anything for the rhyme's sake.

Throughout his career Swinburne published literary criticism of great worth. His deep knowledge of world literatures contributed to a critical style rich in quotation, allusion, and comparison. He is particularly noted for discerning studies of Elizabethan dramatists and of many English and French poets and novelists. As well he was a noted essayist and wrote two novels.

Swinburne was nominated for the Nobel Prize in Literature every year from 1903 to 1907 and then again in 1909.

H.P. Lovecraft, the master of the dark side and a decent poet himself, considered Swinburne "the only real poet in either England or America after the death of Mr. Edgar Allan Poe."

Swinburne was also responsible for devising a poetic form called the roundel, a variation of the French Rondeau form. In 1883 he published A Century of Roundels with several of the roundels dedicated to Dante's sister, the poet Christina Georgina Rossetti. Swinburne wrote to Edward Burne-Jones in 1883: "I have got a tiny new book of songs or songlets, in one form and all manner of metres ... just coming out, of which Miss Rossetti has accepted the dedication. I hope you and Georgie [his wife Georgiana] will find something to like among a hundred poems of nine lines each, twenty-four of which are about babies or small children".

Opinions of the Roundel poems move between those who find them captivating and brilliant, to others who find them merely clever and contrived. One of them, A Baby's Death, was set to music by the English composer Sir Edward Elgar as the song "Roundel: The little eyes that never knew Light".

After the first Poems and Ballads, Swinburne's later poetry was devoted more to philosophy and politics, including the unification of Italy, particularly in the volume Songs before Sunrise. He did not stop writing love poetry entirely, indeed it was only in 1882 that his great epic-length poem, Tristram of Lyonesse, was published, its contents lyrical rather than shocking. His versification, and especially his rhyming technique, remain of high quality to the end.

Algernon Charles Swinburne died of influenza, at the Pines in London on April 10th, 1909 at the age of 72. He was buried at St. Boniface Church, Bonchurch on the Isle of Wight.

Algernon Charles Swinburne – A Concise Bibliography

Verse Drama
The Queen Mother (1860)
Rosamond (1860)
Chastelard (1865)
Bothwell (1874)
Mary Stuart (1881)
Marino Faliero (1885)
Locrine (1887)
The Sisters (1892)
Rosamund, Queen of the Lombards (1899)

Poetry
Atalanta in Calydon (1865)*
Poems and Ballads (1866)
Songs Before Sunrise (1871)
Songs of Two Nations (1875)
Erechtheus (1876)*
Poems and Ballads, Second Series (1878)
Songs of the Springtides (1880)
Studies in Song (1880)
The Heptalogia, or the Seven against Sense. A Cap with Seven Bells (1880)
Tristram of Lyonesse (1882)
A Dark Month & Other Poems
A Century of Roundels (1883)
A Midsummer Holiday and Other Poems (1884)
Poems and Ballads, Third Series (1889)
Astrophel and Other Poems (1894)
The Tale of Balen (1896)
A Channel Passage and Other Poems (1904)

*Although formally tragedies, Atlanta in Calydon and Erechtheus are traditionally included with his poetry.

Criticism
William Blake: A Critical Essay (1868, new edition 1906)
Under the Microscope (1872)
George Chapman: A Critical Essay (1875)
Essays and Studies (1875)
A Note on Charlotte Brontë (1877)
A Study of Shakespeare (1880)
A Study of Victor Hugo (1886)
A Study of Ben Johnson (1889)
Studies in Prose and Poetry (1894)

The Age of Shakespeare (1908)
Shakespeare (1909)

Major Collections
The Poems of Algernon Charles Swinburne, 6 vols. 1904.
The Tragedies of Algernon Charles Swinburne, 5 vols. 1905.
The Complete Works of Algernon Charles Swinburne, 20 vols. Bonchurch Edition. 1925-7.
The Swinburne Letters, 6 vols. 1959-62.

www.ingramcontent.com/pod-product-compliance
Lightning Source LLC
Chambersburg PA
CBHW060059050426
42448CB00011B/2533